SPACE BUSTERS

SPACE MYSTERIES

Steve Parker

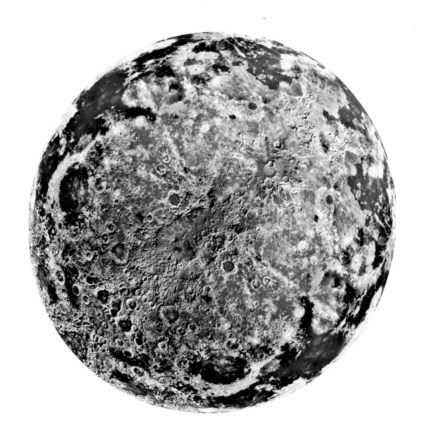

Belitha Press

LOOK FOR THE BIG BANG

Look out for boxes like this with the Big Bang in the corner. They contain extra information and amazing space-buster facts and figures.

Produced by
Monkey Puzzle Media Ltd,
Gissing's Farm, Fressingfield,
Suffolk IP21 5SH, UK

First published in the UK in 2002 by
Belitha Press Limited
An imprint of Chrysalis Books plc,
64 Brewery Road,
London N7 9NT, UK

Designer: Tessa Barwick
Editor: Susan Behar
Consultant: Stuart Atkinson

ISBN 1 84138 367 8

British Library Cataloguing in Publication Data for this book is available from the British Library.

Printed in Hong Kong
10 9 8 7 6 5 4 3 2 1

Acknowledgements
We wish to thank the following individuals and organizations for their help and assistance and for supplying material in their collections: Camera Press 20 (N Prommer); Corbis 12 bottom (Aaron Horowitz); 22 top (Roger Ressmeyer); Kobal Collection 22 bottom; MPM Images front cover, back cover top, bottom left and bottom right, 1, 2, 5 both, 6, 7 top, 9 both, 11, 13, 14, 15 top, 17, 19 both, 21 both, 23, 26, 27, 28, 29, 31; NASA 4; Science Photo Library 3 (Mehau Kulyk), 7 bottom (Fred McConnaughey), 8 (Mehau Kulyk), 10, 12 top (NRAO), 15 top (Luke Dodd), 15 bottom (Françoise Sauze), 16 (Sheila Terry), 18 (Mehau Kulyk), 24 (Mark Garlick), 25 (Julian Baum). Artwork by Alex Pang.

▼ Space has nothing, not even air. So astronauts wear space suits with air inside. They move around in a jet-powered 'astro-armchair' called the MMU (manned manoeuvring unit).

▶ Did everything, including stars, planets, space and even time, begin in a gigantic explosion called the Big Bang?

CONTENTS

How Far is Space?

Space begins about 100 kilometres above the ground. It would take one hour to get there in a fast car that went straight up. Hundreds of people have been into space. The farthest that anyone has travelled is to the Moon.

The Moon is about 384 000 kilometres away. If you could drive there in a car, it would take half a year. Spacecraft go so fast, it takes astronauts less than three days. Even so, the Moon is hardly any distance away compared to other places in space.

Between 1969 and 1972, six Apollo spacecraft landed on the Moon. The journey included going around Earth and the Moon many times. So the total trip was well over one million kilometres. It took the space travellers at least eight days.

◄ The only way into space is straight up in a rocket. This Saturn V rocket carried the first astronauts to land on the Moon, in 1969.

Space probes have gone much farther. But they do not carry people. Voyager and Pioneer probes have travelled more than 6000 million kilometres out of our Solar System. But even this is hardly any distance in the vastness of space.

DESTINATION MARS?

After the Moon, the next nearest place in space is Mars. The trip there would take about 6–9 months. Travellers would need to take food, drinks, spacesuits, fuel for the engines and even air to breathe. Once there, they might be able to use Mars' own gases and rocks to help with supplies for the trip back.

▲ High above Earth, the Hubble Space Telescope peers deep into space.

▼ Space probes can travel to the farthest planets of the Solar System and beyond.

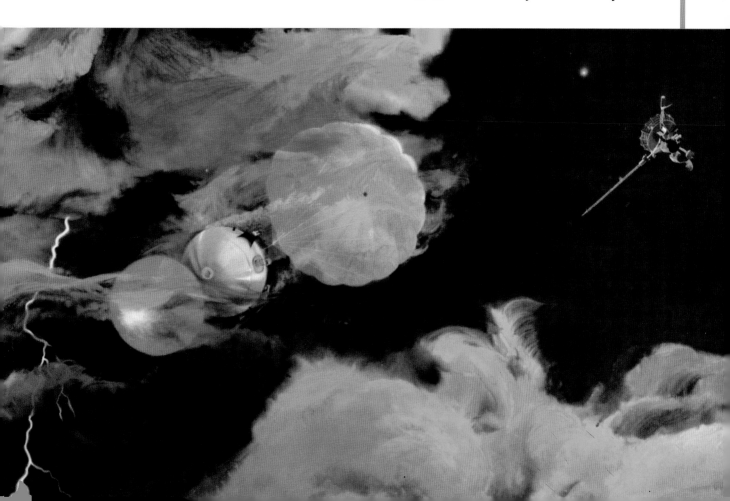

ALL ABOUT THE SUN

The Sun is a star – a giant ball of burning gas. It is so big that more than one million Earths would fit inside. Compared to the size of space, the Sun is very near to us. It is only 150 million kilometres away. If you could fly to the Sun in a jet plane, it would take 18 years!

The Sun has been shining for five billion years. What will happen to it in the future, as it gets older? Looking at other stars of different ages, far away in space, scientists can make a good guess.

▼ The Sun's surface is covered by bubbles of fire. Now and then, giant loops of flames, thousands of times bigger than Earth, leap into space.

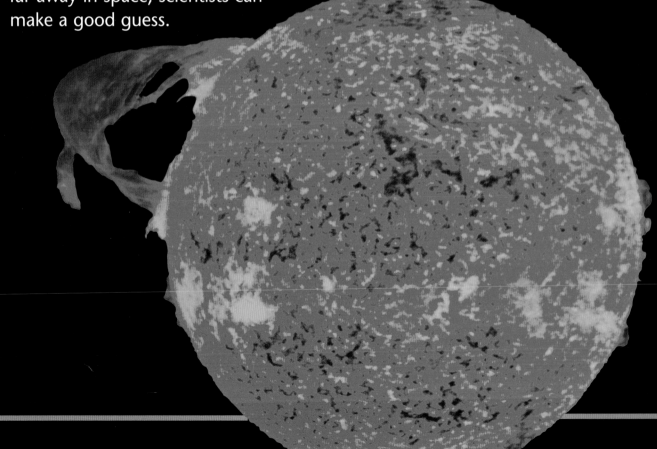

First, the Sun will probably shine for another five billion years. So we do not have to worry about it going out just yet. But then, the Sun may get bigger, brighter and hotter. It may grow so huge that it almost touches Earth. If there is still life here, it will be scorched and even burned.

▲ A furnace for melting metal seems hot to us. But it is hardly warm compared to the heat of the Sun.

Then the Sun will slowly shrink, but still stay very hot. Finally, after billions more years, the Sun will run out of heat. It will end up cold and dark.

◄ Light from the Sun makes trees and plants grow, and supports life on Earth.

HOW HOT IS THE SUN?

The surface of the Sun is more than five times hotter than a fire here on Earth. The middle of the Sun is 15 000 times hotter – an incredible 15 million degrees! We know how hot the Sun is from its colour, and by measuring its heat as it passes through space.

EXPLODING STARS

A star begins as a vast cloud of gas and dust, called a nebula, floating in space. Everything, including a nebula, is affected by a force called gravity which pulls things together. Even tiny specks of dust and gas have gravity. In space, where they can move easily, they gradually come closer to each other.

▼ A star that blows up, as a supernova, is far brighter than a thousand Suns.

The gravity in the nebula pulls its pieces together into a lump. As the lump forms, it gathers enough energy to burn at its centre. It becomes a star and starts to shine.

A small star, like our Sun, shines for millions of years. It may swell up even more and become a red giant. Gradually it becomes smaller, but it still shines for a time. It is then called a white dwarf.

A big star keeps growing. It becomes a red supergiant, hundreds of times larger than our Sun. It gets even bigger, and hotter, until one day – BANG! It blows up like a massive space-bomb. This is known as a supernova.

▲ A volcano is a tiny version of an exploding star.

▶ An exploding star blasts some of itself far into space. The central part is small and soon cools.

✳ IS A WHITE DWARF HEAVY?

Very. It contains all the gas, dust and matter from a giant star, pressed into an object the size of a planet like Earth. A piece of white dwarf as big as a pea would weigh more than a whole mountain.

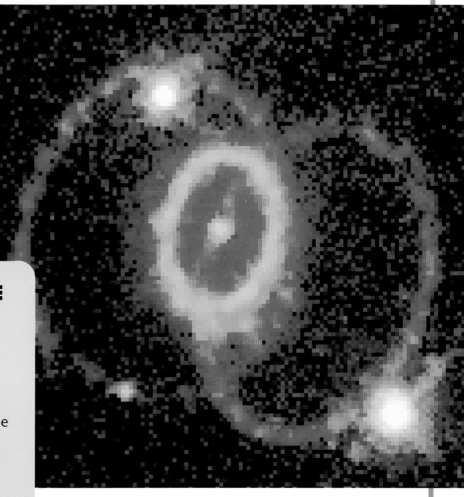

THE MILKY WAY

▲ This is Quintuplet Cluster, a group of stars near the centre of the Milky Way. It contains the brightest star in our galaxy, called the Pistol star.

You can see a pale streak across the dark night sky on some nights. This is called the Milky Way. It is a huge, narrow group of stars, stretching into deep space, with fewer stars on either side.

Stars are not spread evenly through space. They are in groups or clumps which are called galaxies. Our Sun is in a galaxy called the Milky Way. The Milky Way is flat and round, like a plate, but with a bulge in the middle.

As we look at the Milky Way, we see a narrow band of billions of stars stretching away across the sky – a bit like a plate hanging in space. As we look to either side, it's like looking above and below the plate. There are fewer stars and there is more empty space.

The Milky Way has at least 100 billion stars. There are millions of other galaxies, and each one has billions of stars too. Between the galaxies are great empty regions of nothing.

HOW DO WE SEE INTO SPACE?

Astronomers have used telescopes for hundreds of years to study the sky. A telescope is like a very powerful human eye that makes objects seem bigger and brighter than they are. Scientists have discovered a lot of facts about our Galaxy using telescopes on Earth and in space.

▶ Radio telescopes do not collect light for us to see. They collect invisible waves such as radio waves and microwaves. A computer changes the waves into a picture for us to study.

PULSARS AND QUASARS

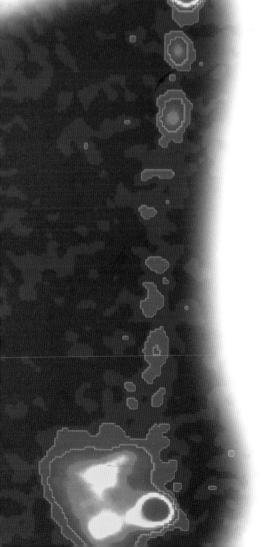

▼ This quasar, 1007+417, shoots out giant blobs of ultra-hot gases.

One day in 1967 scientists tuned into strange signals from space. They were radio waves in bursts or pulses. They went 'beep-beep-beep' without stopping. Were they from aliens trying to contact Earth?

No. Scientists worked out that the radio signals came from a special kind of star called a pulsar. This is a very old, cold, dead star. The radio waves mainly come out of one side of the pulsar. Pulsars, like most stars, spin around very fast. So the beam of radio waves goes around in a circle. From far away, it seems to flash on and off like the light beam of a lighthouse.

▲ The light ray from a lighthouse goes around in a circle and seems to flash. Pulsars do the same with radio waves.

A few years before, in 1963, scientists made another amazing discovery. It was something that shines brighter than a billion Suns, yet it is hardly larger than the Sun. It's called a quasar. It is probably the centre of a galaxy, where stars keep crashing together in giant explosions. Scientists have now found hundreds of pulsars and quasars.

▼ Nebulas, such as the Eagle nebula, hide the stars behind them. But the radio waves of pulsars shine straight through.

IS A PULSAR HEAVY?

Yes! A pulsar is even smaller and heavier than a white dwarf star. A small lump of pulsar, the size of a baked bean, weighs more than the whole Earth.

WHAT IS A BLACK HOLE?

WHAT'S A WORMHOLE?

It's like a secret tunnel across space. Its funnel-shaped ends might be near a black hole, or even inside one. If you could get into a wormhole, you would pop out again, far across the Universe. And your trip would take no time at all. But no one knows if wormholes are real.

Nothing can come out of a black hole. In fact, a black hole is black because not even light can escape. But how does a black hole begin, and what might be inside it?

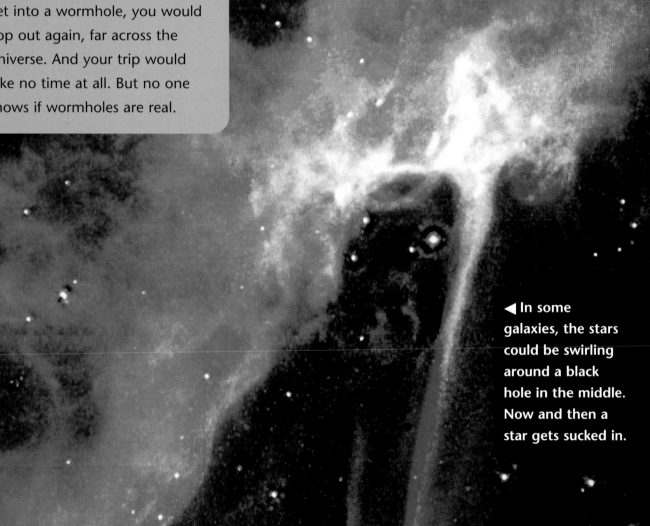

◀ In some galaxies, the stars could be swirling around a black hole in the middle. Now and then a star gets sucked in.

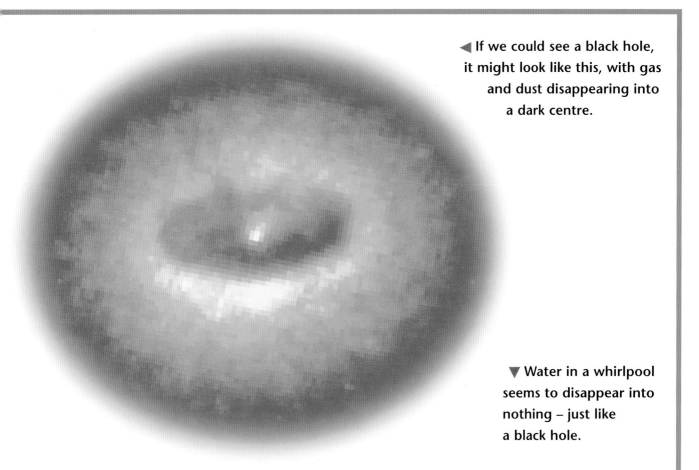

◀ If we could see a black hole, it might look like this, with gas and dust disappearing into a dark centre.

▼ Water in a whirlpool seems to disappear into nothing – just like a black hole.

Everything experiences the pulling force of gravity. A black hole is a place where there is almost too much gravity. This gravity pulls in everything – stars, planets, dust, light and other rays. All of these are squeezed and pressed into a tiny space.

A black hole may start when a giant star explodes as a supernova. Bits of star are left over. They shrink together and drag in nearby stars. As the stars crash together, they give out brilliant flashes of energy. Then the stars, and everything else nearby, swirl around like a whirlpool and disappear into the black hole.

▲ There are too many stars, galaxies and other space objects to count. Yet this is just a tiny corner of the Universe.

THE UNIVERSE!

The Universe is everything. It includes all stars, galaxies, quasars, black holes, dust, gas and everything else, with a lot of empty space between. So how big is all of this?

The Universe is bigger than we could ever imagine. No one even knows its shape. It could be round like a ball, flat like a plate, ring-shaped like a doughnut or an odd shape like a knobbly potato.

▼ People used to think the world looked like this. Today, ideas about the Universe are just as simple.

On Earth, we measure the size of big things in kilometres. In space, kilometres are much too small. Scientists use a measure called the light-year. This is how far light travels in one year. It is 9460 million billion kilometres.

Even a light-year is too small to measure the Universe. Our biggest telescopes can see stars and galaxies which are more than 13 billion light-years away.
Almost certainly, the Universe goes beyond this.
But it's too far for us to see.

▼ To our eyes, the night sky looks dark with twinkling stars. To a radio telescope, which 'sees' other kinds of waves, it looks very bright and colourful.

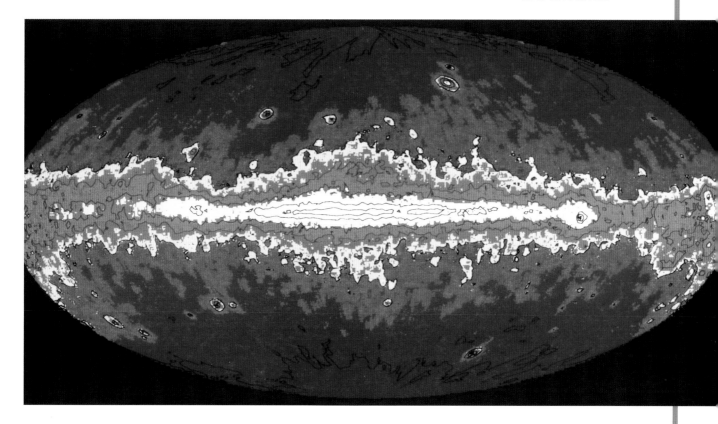

✳ WHAT'S OUTSIDE THE UNIVERSE?

If the Universe is everything, it cannot have an 'outside'. The outside would be part of the Universe too. Some scientists think that outside the Universe is another universe. There might be lots of universes, one inside the other. But no one really knows.

How Did the World Begin?

Scientists argue about whether the Universe ever had a beginning. Maybe it has always been here? In which case, it never started.

▼ The smallest speck could have exploded in the largest explosion ever, as the Universe began with the Big Bang.

This idea is called the Steady State theory. It says that not only did the Universe never begin, but it will never end. And it may change in size, but not much.

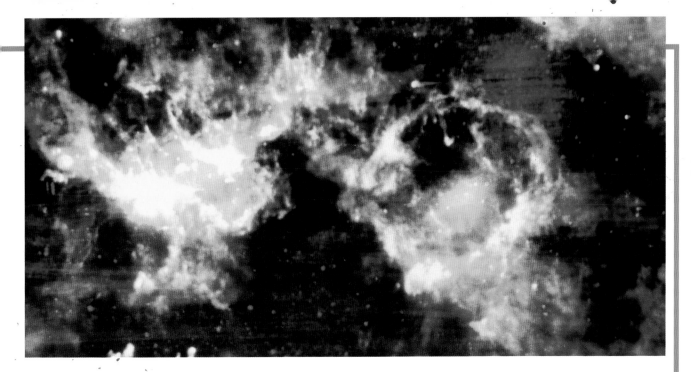

Today most scientists think that the Universe is not in Steady State. Instead it began with a Big Bang. In the beginning, the whole Universe was pressed into a tiny speck. Then a massive explosion blew it apart. Gradually the Universe grew. Galaxies and stars started to form.

If there was a Big Bang, what was before it? One answer is that everything began at the Big Bang. This includes the Universe, and even time itself. If time started at the Big Bang, then you could not go back before it. There was no time to go back into.

▲ Peering deep into space, we are looking back in time at galaxies forming. We see them as they looked billions of years ago.

▼ A computer picture of microwaves in space shows that they are everywhere – left-over from the Big Bang.

 ## IS THE UNIVERSE GROWING?

Yes. The light from distant stars is not quite the same colour as scientists expect. It's more red than it should be. This is called red shift. It shows that stars, galaxies and other objects in space are still flying away from each other, long after the Big Bang.

A Trip to the Stars

▼ Make-believe spacecraft like Star Trek's *USS Voyager* are like cities in space. But could they ever exist?

Modern science says that there is a speed limit. The fastest speed in the whole Universe is the speed of light. Nothing can go faster. If this is true, then we could never travel among the stars.

The speed of light is about 300 000 kilometres each second. So a light beam could go around Earth almost eight times in one second.

◀ An astronaut can live for only a few hours in a spacesuit.

Our nearest star is the Sun. At the speed of light, a trip there would take about eight minutes. In fact, light is making this journey all the time, in the other direction – in the sunlight that travels to Earth.

After the Sun, the next nearest star is Proxima Centauri. At the speed of light, the trip would take about four years. But our spacecraft go hundreds of times slower. So even a trip to Proxima Centauri would take hundreds of years. And most stars are millions of times farther away.

CAN WE BEAT LIGHT SPEED?

Possibly. Imagine you are going on a long journey. By making the journey's distance shorter, you could get there faster. Amazingly, perhaps space could be altered or 'warped' to become smaller. Then you could travel quicker – maybe even faster than light. Many spacecraft in the movies, and on TV, use this idea of 'warp drive'.

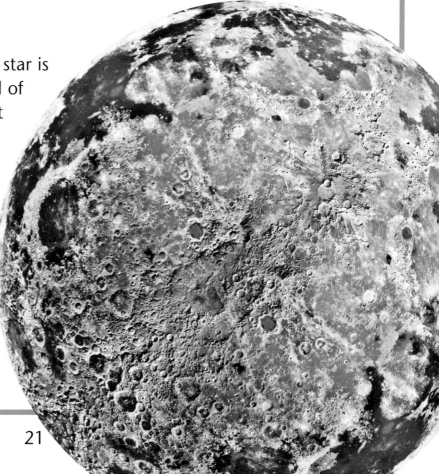

▶ A false-colour photo of the Moon. The Moon is closest to us in space. Even so, it took years to finally get there and it cost a lot of money.

TIME TRAVEL

Time seems to pass in a regular or constant way, always the same. Clocks go tick-tock, tick-tock, tick-tock. But time is not regular. It can speed up or slow down.

Imagine travelling away from Earth and back again in a very fast spacecraft. On landing, the crew say that the trip has taken 10 days. But people on Earth say that the trip has taken 11 days. Both are right. How?

▼ In the *Back to the Future* movies, the time machine used by hero Marty is a sleek sports car with special powers.

▶ The exploding star Supernova 1987A (red spot) blew up long before discoverer Ian Shelton saw it, looking back in time.

SEEING THE PAST?

When we gaze at distant stars, we do not see them as they are today. Their light takes hundreds or thousands of years to reach us. By the time we see it, some of those stars may have blown up or faded away. Looking at the night sky is like looking into the past.

▲ For astronauts in a fast-moving craft, time passes a tiny amount more slowly. When they come back to Earth they are a split-second younger!

As the spacecraft speeds up, its time slows down. The people in the craft would not notice. Their clock ticks as normal. The clocks on Earth also tick. But Earth clocks tick faster, because Earth is moving slower than the spacecraft.

If time goes slower, as speed gets faster, what happens at the speed of light? Perhaps time stands still. If you could go faster than the speed of light, would time go backwards? Maybe.

23

HOW WILL IT ALL END?

▲ Will the whole Universe fall inwards and collapse into a tiny spot, in the Big Crunch?

Many space scientists think that the Universe began as a tiny speck. It exploded in the Big Bang, and got bigger. It's still getting bigger today. Will it carry on like this?

Perhaps. The Universe may continue to grow, partly because it has so much empty space. The more space, the less gravity the objects have, so the galaxies will keep moving farther apart and the Universe will keep getting larger and larger.

But some scientists say that there is enough gravity in the Universe to stop it getting bigger forever. Perhaps it will gradually slow down, and then stay at the same size.

Another idea is that the Universe will stop getting bigger, and start to get smaller. Finally it will be so small that the whole Universe is squeezed into a tiny speck. This is the opposite of the Big Bang. It's known as the Big Crunch.

No one knows the truth. But scientists have amazing ideas as they try to solve the mysteries of space.

HOW LONG IS FOREVER?

Time itself may have started at the Big Bang. When the Big Crunch comes, time may stop. There was no 'before' the Big Bang, and there will be no 'after' the Big Crunch.

▼ The *Voyager 2* space probe left the planets of our Solar System in 1989. With almost nothing in the way it may speed through space forever.

SPACE-MYSTERY FACTS

Here are some interesting space facts and figures.

Mysterious visitors

Comets are rare visitors to our tiny part of space. Each has a small, shiny head with a vast, long, glowing tail. Ancient people watched comets with wonder and fear. Were they spaceships of the gods? Did they bring terrible evil and disaster?

No longer mysterious

We now know that a comet is a small ball of very cold rock, ice and crystals. It travels on a long, lop-sided orbit around the Sun. As it nears the Sun's warmth, its tail grows longer. One of the most famous comets is Halley's Comet, which returns every 76 years.

▶ In 2001 the *Mir* space station fell back to Earth.

Flashing stars

Some stars seem to shine brighter, then dimmer, as though flashing or winking on and off. Some of these are binaries – two stars close together, going around each other. When we see the two stars come together, their light adds together, so they look like one star getting brighter.

Bouncing Universe

If the Universe keeps getting bigger after a Big Bang, then collapsing again in a Big Crunch, how long does all this take? One view is that the Universe makes a 'bounce' once every 80 billion years.

First black hole

In the 1970s, space scientist Stephen Hawking suggested that black holes could actually be real. The first black holes were found in the early 1990s.

Shining Sun

The brightness of a star is called its magnitude. The Sun is very bright, with a magnitude of –26.8 (the lower the magnitude the brighter the star). But that's mainly because the Sun is so near to Earth. Compared to many other stars, it's not that bright.

Sirius A
The next brightest star, when seen from Earth, is Sirius A, which is in the star group called Canis Major. Its magnitude is minus 1.47 and it is more than eight light-years away.

Brightest star
The brightest known star is called Cygnus OB2/12. It shines nearly one million times brighter than the Sun.

Alpha Orionis
The biggest star is Alpha Orionis, also called Betelgeuse. It is 310 light-years away and is about 500 times wider than the Sun.

Age of the Universe
Most scientists think that the Universe is between 12 000 million and 14 000 million years old. But it could be 20 000 million years of age.

Heaviest star
The star called Eta Carinae may be almost 200 times heavier than the Sun.

Size of the Universe
No one knows how big the Universe is, or even if it has an edge. It could simply go on forever. The most distant objects we can see from Earth are galaxies more than 13 billion light-years away.

▲ The International Space Station is being built far above our heads to replace the *Mir* space station.

SPACE-MYSTERY WORDS

astronaut
The American name for someone who has travelled into space.

Big Bang
The event when the Universe, and even time itself, may have begun.

Big Crunch
The event when the Universe, and time itself, may end. It would be like the reverse of the Big Bang, when the whole Universe squeezes and shrinks back to almost nothing.

galaxy
A group of stars which are quite close together, with great amounts of empty space all around. There are usually millions of stars in a galaxy.

gravity
A pulling or attracting force. Everything has gravity, and the bigger the object is, the stronger its gravity. Earth's gravity pulls us down on to its surface. A star has massive gravity that can bend light rays.

light-year
A measure of distance, not time. It is the distance travelled by light in one year, which is about 9460 million billion kilometres.

Milky Way
The name for our galaxy, or group of stars. It is also just called 'the galaxy'. It contains about 100 billion stars, the nearest one to us being the Sun.

nebula
A vast cloud of gas and dust floating in space. Some nebulas gradually get smaller and clump together to form stars.

planet
An object which goes around, or orbits, a star. Our own star, the Sun, has nine planets, making up the Solar System. Earth is the third planet from the Sun.

pulsar
An old, small, heavy, fast-spinning star, also called a neutron star. It sends out regular bursts or pulses of radio waves.

quasar
One of the brightest of all objects in space. Quasars may be the centres of galaxies, where stars crash together before they disappear into a black hole.

▼ Some galaxies like our own Milky Way, are shaped like spirals or whirlpools.

▶ The *Pioneer* space probe is one of the most distant of all probes.

red giant
A star which is much bigger than the Sun and which glows with a reddish light. Our Sun may become a red giant in a few billion years.

red shift
When light from stars and other distant objects looks redder than it should do. The effect is caused by the star moving away at great speed.

Solar System
The Sun, the nine planets which go around it (including Earth) and other nearby bits of rock and gas, including comets and asteroids.

space
Everywhere which is not Earth. Most of space is empty. It is dotted with tiny specks which are stars and other objects.

spacecraft
A craft or vehicle which can travel into space, carrying people. It is powered by a rocket engine and designed to keep the people alive and healthy, and to bring them safely back to Earth.

space probe
A machine or device, for exploring space, which does not carry people. It is controlled by radio signals sent from Earth, and it sends back radio signals about what it has found.

speed of light
The distance that light travels in a certain time. It is about 300 000 kilometres in one second. Nothing can go faster than light – probably.

star
An object in space that shines with incredibly hot, burning gases. A star gives off light, heat and many types of rays and waves.

supernova
A huge star that suddenly explodes. For a few days or weeks, it shines brighter than 100 million Suns. Then it fades away as small pieces.

Universe
Everything there is – all the space, stars, planets, galaxies and everything else. It includes all the things we know about, and even all the things we can only imagine.

white dwarf
A star which is near the end of its life. It is old and small, perhaps only the size of Earth. But it still shines, maybe even hotter than the Sun. In many millions of years the Sun will probably become a white dwarf.

wormhole
A 'tunnel' across space and through time. Its ends are in different parts of the Universe. If wormholes are real, they may be one way to travel between the stars, and even go back or forwards in time.

SPACE-MYSTERY PROJECTS

▼ The Universe is getting bigger, just like a blown-up balloon. The star clusters or galaxies are moving farther apart, like the spots on the balloon.

EXPANDING UNIVERSE

You can show how the Universe is probably getting bigger by blowing up a balloon! First, use a thick-pointed marker pen to put some dark spots on the balloon. These will be galaxies of stars. Imagine that the balloon is the Universe when it began. Now start the Big Bang – blow up the balloon. It expands just like the real Universe.

See how the spots get bigger and also farther apart. This is happening with real galaxies, as they grow in size and move away from each other.

A TRIP TO MARS!

Imagine that you are going to the planet Mars. You have to make a list of all the things to take in your spacecraft. But there is not much room, so you can only take what you really need. Start at the beginning:

- Air to breathe
- Water and other drinks
- Spacesuit to wear outside
- Food to eat
- Clothes to wear
- Exercise bike to keep fit
- Anything else?

DANGER – BLACK HOLE?

What do you think it might look like in a black hole? One idea is that objects become long and thin. It's called 'spaghetti-fication'. Draw a picture of this, as you imagine that you and your craft swirl towards the centre of a huge black hole.

SPACE ADVENTURERS

Now that you have read this book, try testing your knowledge. Next time you watch a movie or TV programme about space, see if you are able to work out what is make-believe in the story and what is based on science and facts.

STAR-GAZERS

People who study stars, planets and what happens in space are known as astronomers. Each country has its own astronomy society. There are also many smaller astronomy groups.

▼ How long will it be before humans can really go on a mission to Mars?

SPACE INTERNET SITES
Virtual trips in space

antwrp.gsfc.nasa.gov/htmltest/rjn_bht.html

This website shows pictures of what you might see in a black hole, or next to a pulsar. You may find the words quite difficult but the pictures are very good.

NASA and Space

NASA, the USA's National Aeronautics and Space Administration, gives us much of our information about space. NASA has many Internet sites. Some are designed for younger people.

NASA for Kids
www.nasa.gov/kids.html

The Space Place
spaceplace.jpl.nasa.gov

Space Kids
www.spacekids.com

INDEX